THE
NAMES
of
BIRDS

ALSO BY TOM CRAWFORD

I Want to Say Listen
If It Weren't for Trees
Lauds
China Dancing
The Temple on Monday
Wu Wei

THE
NAMES
of BIRDS

POEMS BY

Tom Crawford

SHERMAN ASHER PUBLISHING
Santa Fe

ISBN: 978-1-890932-40-4

Library of Congress Control Number: 2011913879

Sherman Asher Publishing

126 Candelario St.

Santa Fe, NM 87501

www.shermanasher.com

Manufactured in the U.S.A.

For Mary

CONTENTS

Foreword by David James Duncan   11

SECTION I

It's Such a Relief to Want Less   17

For the Certain Dark Days   18

Wing   19

Cowbird   22

The Toll Birds Take   24

Family: Troglodytidae   26

To Make an Owl Make a Poem   28

Water Ouzel   30

The Objective Case of Who   31

I'm Sixty-two   33

The Enthusiast   34

Bushtit   35

Bobcat Bite   36

Steel Cut   39

Going Out   40

Birders   42

Where the Country Goes Wrong   44

Christopher Columbus Discovers
    the Tar Sands of Alberta   46

Outsider Art   48

Wasn't My Arm a Wing?   51

All the Birds Are Here   53

Harriet   55

The Morandi Gaze   57

SECTION II

Great Word   61

Companion to a Loon   63

Heavy Lifting   64

Gray Lodge   65

Half a Buddha   66

Crop Circles   67

Release at Netarts Bay   75

Roosevelt's Diary   77

What's Christmas to a Bird   81

Spotter Scope   83

Rain   85

Pigeon Guillemot   86

Crack Corn   87

Redwing   88

Am I My Feet?   89

"Tender Your Resignation"   90

Prayer   91

Bird Walk in China   93

Wu Wei   95

SECTION III

Arrhythmia   99

The Names of Birds   101

It Hands Out the Gold   103

Feeder   104

Not Being a God   105

On the Back Side of a Cemetery in Santa Fe, NM   108

One Bird Works for a While   109

Yellow-breasted Chat   111

The Chinese Might Say,
    There Is No Tea in You   113

In Order to Let the Soul Out Sooner   114

Cello   116

To Remember, Again, What's Good   118

Grackle   120

Raptor   122

The President's Last Speech   124

What Lasts   126

To Go Very Softly   127

The Pie Is *Now*   129

Raven   130

The Spill   132

Ownership   133

Bosque del Apache   135

Canary   137

The Good Red Road   138

Acknowledgments   140

FOREWORD

Peering Back

As I write these words, birds are migrating en masse, north through the Gulf States, while a Senate hearing is being conducted on the BP oil spill. Television covers half the story. Unseen suffering covers the other half. The whole story goes something like this: fabulously rich oil execs deserve Oscars for their struggles to appear sincere as they tell us they're not responsible for the drilling rigs that enriched them—while Brown Pelicans regurgitate four gallons of oily water after each attempt to catch a fish. Lobbyist-fattened senators, having long ago approved the drilling, placate their sponsoring oilmen while Black Skimmers jet their bills through fatal slicks. Hoping their pricey suits will lend them an air of refinement, the execs and pols do manage to achieve the look of the refined flour used in balloon bread.

"Senate hearing." Nice term for the deafness that leaves Royal Terns mewing in flightless huddles till they drop to the blackened sand; Ruddy Turnstones flipping oil-balls they've mistaken for rocks; Magnificent Frigatebirds with seven foot wingspans, oil-grounded for life, slipping slowly into shock.

"Human beings are spiritual animals," Tom Crawford once wrote, "and to forget this is to invite calamity. Words empty of meaning, poetry vanishes, birds become 'species' occupying 'habitat,' their 'decline' due to 'environmental causes.' Not so. It's the human spirit that's in decline. It's our loss of wonder, our disconnect from the planet, that endangers life. A great raven peers down as it floats over our heads, black wing feathers shining. To fail to peer back is to forsake what humans and ravens are meant to be."

Most of the ravens in my home valley near Lolo Montana peer down from hundreds of feet overhead. As an acolyte in Tom's First Church of Birds, I rush out at the sound of their calls anyhow, calling back in what I hope is their language. And if I've got a cold, so there's a little googy in my throat, they sometimes spiral down in search of the unidentified caller. What good-humored *klooks* they then make when they spot featherless, flightless me. Do they know I'm a hoax from the start? Do they appreciate my efforts even so? Hard to say, in English. But in the Church of Birds we hold that ravens peering and calling down, and humans peering and calling back, are the only safeguards we have against devastations like the one sweeping the Gulf.

Birds live with an integrity and courage that elude humans, but when we make room for them in our lives their integrity and courage awaken our own. Tom Crawford's bird poems are a compendium of bird/human interaction in all their sometimes—inglorious glory. Small travesties against small lives; small acts of service toward small lives; anything but small awakenings. Tom's long attention to birds involves us in magic, but no hocus pocus: it's simply impossible, these poems quietly insist, to be feathered and fail to dazzle; impossible to own wings and not transcend. Jesus' words *"Consider the fowls of the air"* is not a complicated commandment in Tom's mind. When the male goldfinch and Lazuli Bunting dress to the nines to *wow* a female, he too cries *Wow!* When the Bar-tailed Godwit flies six thousand nautical miles in six days without resting, Tom rightfully gasps *Holy shit!* When the Steller's Jay mimics the redtail trying to sound like a badass or the starling mimics the bobwhite to feign the innocence it lacks, Tom too is moved to imitation—and so resorts to the language of poetry.

The result is a very ancient, very powerful form of exchange. The solace birds embody via song, plumage, and behavior is almost unchanging in a world of sickeningly rapid change. Every clear moment of bird-to-human contact touches a place in us beyond space and time. Nothing has changed, for instance, since the 8th century moment that inspired Li Po to write:

> *The birds have vanished down the sky*
> *and now the last cloud drains away.*
> *We sit together, the mountain and me*
> *til only the mountain remains.*

Nothing has changed since the 13th century moment that moved Dogen to say:

> *The migrating bird*
> *leaves no trace behind*
> *'and does not need a guide*

Nothing has changed since the 20th century instant that caused Rilke to write:

> *The inner—what is it*
> *if not the intensified sky,*
> *hurled through with birds?*

The sky never ages, and birds and poems, all their lives, pierce this timelessness. The sky makes room for sunlight, thunderheads, F-16's, the concertos of Mozart, the blat of Senate Gulf oil spill hearings, the killing sprays of Monsanto and spume of Big Coal, the bemused tunes of small children forging a life amid the spume, and birds and poems move all their lives through this spaciousness. Birds save nothing, carry nothing, live song to song, seed to seed, sky to mouth, calling to a place beyond our day to day sense of limits—and so do the prayers imbedded in these poems.

Tom's response to birds is the Denise Levertov response:

Those who were sacred have remained so.
Holiness does not dissolve, it is a presence
of bronze, only the sight that saw it
faltered and turned from it.
An old joy returns in holy presence.

"What Seymour loved most about the Bible" wrote J.D. Salinger, "was the word, '*Watch!*'" Year in and year out, Tom Crawford keeps doing so.

A great raven peers down, black wing feathers shining.
Open this book and peer back.
An old joy returns with these poems.

—DAVID JAMES DUNCAN

SECTION I

What is fate but the density of childhood.

—RAINER MARIA RILKE

IT'S SUCH A RELIEF TO WANT LESS

It's such a relief to want less.
Let the Sharp-shinned Hawk who is not greedy
so eats only one small sparrow a day
be my model, right down to the wing
picked joints and the tidy pile of gray feathers
the wind soon blows away. Nobody
in my family learned the quiet habit
of bird watching. We weren't in one place
long enough for a feeder, for the songs
our own silence might bring.
Age comes swift,
but my eyesight only gets better.
No tragedy in my backyard.
No props.
No villains.
There is no such thing,
you know, as a sick old hawk.

FOR THE CERTAIN DARK DAYS

The angel that might
knock you off your horse
on the way
into the noisy city
is no match for the tanager
landing on the suet.
You'll look in vain
to find him anywhere
in the Gospels. Not one
parable about the necessity
for beauty if we are to go on.

All these books,
talk shows
about dying.

Breeding plumage
to dazzle the female
into making more birds
like this one should have us
all running to put up more
peanut butter.

WING

When I was eleven
I found a black wing,
just one wing,
on our road.

I was a loner.
Shy. Afraid a lot.

For a long time
I kept it in my pocket.

If I was really nervous
I'd take it out
and fan it open
like a deck of cards.

Or I'd throw it up
in the air like it was
a whole bird
when a flock
of whistling
blackbirds
flew over.

The feathers
glowed green,
all ten of them,
if I held them
up to the sun

and turned it
just right.

After a while
I wore it
around my neck,
with a white string
tied to the bone.

I'd only take it off
when there was a bully
around.

Then one day
my dad looked
at me,
and told me
I was making
too much of it.

Where the water
spilled over the weir
in the canal
behind our farm,
I let it go. A swirl
in the current
by the bank caught
the white string
and my feathers,
pulling them out
past the snake grass

and into the fast water.

At the time
it seemed alright.
The water
was a comfort to me.
My wing
was going
somewhere
I believed
to a better life.

COWBIRD

Jesus didn't take hold when I was young.
I'd skip church and use my donation
for bubble gum. If there was a divine spark
it was the cowbird scratching in the feedlot
at Paiute Packing Company on Wible Road,
metallic green with intense brown head,
it'd get right down in the molasses and oats
with those sweet-breathed cows being fattened
for slaughter. Row on row of White-faced,
Angus, Holstein, their heads moving up and down
in the morning sun, in the grain. The little bird
would step carefully around the cow's wet
nose, fat tongue as the animal stretched it out
to pull in more feed. I knew what the background
noise meant, the grating sound of the chains,
the cursing human voices, the white steam
blowing through the vents, and the sounds
of the bellowing cows coming through
the walls. On the other side they came out
in quarters, frozen, on the shoulders of big men
in red smeared white coats who loaded them
into trucks backed up to the dock. What matters,
growing up didn't really take either. Yesterday
in Whole Foods in Santa Fe, New Mexico, sixty years

later, I'm bent over the counter picking up packages
of organically grown beef, reading the labels
to find out what part of the cow I'm holding.
I'm seeing in the reflective cellophane the asses
of cows going up the shit-caked ramp that narrows
then leads them single file into the slaughter house,
their long tails swishing away flies.
Sometimes a cowbird rides one up on its back,
walking nervously along the spine, then flies off
at the last moment when the big metal door
slides open.

THE TOLL BIRDS TAKE

You have to understand the toll birds take,
perched or on the wing
concentrated beauty is a war of nerves.
One can enter you from any direction
and a fly-through, even by the common sparrow,
can take out the heart.
That's the nature of ambush,
something that lies in wait: a nuthatch
walking perpendicular
down a tree, dressed to kill,
ruined me for years. Now
I take precautions, cover my eyes
to the Wood Duck, stand back
from the window in winter
when the chickadees come to feed.
Snow is a bad thing where any birds gather,
so much color is always a show of force.
Look at the ancient crow,
a black glove on the landscape,
one finger always mocking you.
He was ugly, but when Herby Poole
stood up in class in the eighth grade
and imitated the songs of several birds,
including the difficult vireo,

we were never the same.
That was years ago and he died,
don't birds die, birds above all things
who unnerve us just in passing,
who leave us breathless and sad?

FAMILY: TROGLODYTIDAE

All this praise for the missile
and none for the little wren
that goes in bursts of flight
from rock to brush
to creek without forethought
or plan. It doesn't seem to know
beforehand where it will dine
or when. We don't know,
either, if it dreams spiders
on its plate. Or in matters of love
which of its shy notes
might lure another in?
War is out of the question,
though, if behavior is any clue,
since it avoids other birds, people.
Propelled partly by its erect tail,
it lives close to the earth
and will nest only in something dark,
a knothole, a discarded boot.
It just wants to make more
wrens and leave it at that.
I know I'm a bad ornithologist.
I bring no data: maps or distribution
of species or description of habitat,

only me, following my feelings in
the side of what can't be
replaced. It's my job, though,
in a loud world. To be quiet.
Friend to the smallest song.

TO MAKE AN OWL MAKE A POEM

No tools required.
Not so hard if you start small,
say with the beak
which is entirely manageable,
pinching a little ball of soft stoneware
between the tool of your thumb
and index finger
the head begins to sprout
from the spontaneous eyes
the tips of the fingers
just naturally make
so you see immediately
where the broad shoulders
want to begin.

To make an owl
is to forget yourself,
the coins in your pockets,
failed love,
the fame you'll never have.

To make an owl make a poem
you have to
be very nearly out of control

in the squish and push
and pull of it
to make a poem
stand up
solitary
for you like that
and be an owl.

WATER OUZEL

Maybe it's from moss
he gets the green light
to walk under water. In Paul's letter
to the Ephesians, he's almost mentioned,
but who would believe in the miracle
of a little bird, especially standing
in white water, peering
down around his own feet
for food while the creek flows
over. "Down there" is always subjective,
but you can watch him
descend in a zigzag walk
down to where light sets the table.
Small himself, it's the spineless
he's after. What we want to
figure out, he eats. How many feet
of creek does it take, for example,
to make one Ouzel? What feeling is
to poetry, larvae is to caddis—a sudden hatch—
the porch light by the screen door
where hundreds hang on.
We have to be content
to name what he brings up: hellgrammite,
nymph, stone fly.

THE OBJECTIVE CASE OF WHO

My millet, my seeds, they'll eat right on
through winter but no mail ever comes
expressing appreciation from them
for having to forage less when the snow flies.

So, the objective case of who
doesn't mean squat when it comes to
man or bird: who needs whom the most?

I suppose it's humility, (Can you say that
in a poem?), how small I am, too
in the bird's-eye view of things
when you add it all up

billions of dollars later and years
to build the Collider, yet we're only left
with probability as to which way
the little bird might fly.

I can't help it, though, like the old physicist,
I too believe in the divine order of things,

so I hold my finger out for the tiny vireo
at the feeder with the hope that it will

come over, that's right
and light on it.

God bless gravity though,
the way it throws us all a curve
on the round earth,
and puts spring in the poem.

I'M SIXTY-TWO

Another day ignorant.
Here comes the sun anyway.
So beautiful I could just pee my pants.
Frost wore diapers after seventy
his daughter told his biographer
he'd get so excited.
It doesn't get easier.
I just filleted a yellow perch
I caught an hour ago in the bay.
Its long gut unfolded
like origami,
one sand shrimp after another.
You see what I mean?
I live alone to spare myself,
another, the intensity of feelings
even a little bird brings on,
eating the bread crumbs
I put out the night before.

THE ENTHUSIAST

Mine was a coarse intelligence,
I knew that, a man
upon whom nuance was wasted.
Clay in my hands
did not refine itself
into anything more than a dog head
that could also be a pig head—
you could choose—vessels
good for nothing, my pinch pots
closed off to meaning
or the thick, squat stupas
I'd made, devotional, the way I imagined
a hunkered down Buddha.
In the end my heart
still banging out those small notes
I could not hear.
An enthusiast, that's what I was,
big knuckled, splitter of wood,
guffawer of the dumb joke,
enchanted always by the obvious—
birds, yes, especially birds,
the pigeon-toed crow,
clumsy in its deportment,
who had no particular song
but who did not want to be anything else.

BUSHTITS

all
in under
a few
seconds
like a little
platoon
of Roman
soldiers
appear,
what surprise
when they
suddenly
rush
the suet
so it swings
wildly
on its chain,
seven
gray birds,
beaks
like spears
driving
into the fat,
heads,
helmets
tossing.

BOBCAT BITE

In here you want to sing
"Joy to the World" in June.
The young waitress' smile
makes you feel young again
like if you order the buffalo
burger with green chili,
she comes with it.

Sitting at the wooden
counter, peering out
the big window
right in front of me
is like being in the Museum
of Natural History
on Central Park West
only the birds
are alive. The blue Pinyon Jay
hangs upside-down
to get at the seed bag
while I'm trying to swallow
too big a bite from my burger,
catsup juice dripping
through my fingers.

Birds can make you not care
about who's watching you,
grease running down your chin.

I have favorites.

A little Hermit Thrush arrives.
Sips water, and then holds its head
up to swallow. Its song,
I remember, a long, plaintive whistle,
sadly fading at the end,
saved me young.

With the window small,
there's only four seats
for bird watching at Bobcat Bite,
so it's like waiting in line
to see Vermeer's *Milkmaid*.
All worth it.

I wrote it down
so I wouldn't forget.
On April 3rd, last year
I saw the rare Cactus Wren
and blurted it out
to the whole café

with part of my hamburger,
all the time pointing
at the window.

One time an old man
sitting next to me, a tourist,
from St. Paul said he'd heard
about Bobcat Bite
from his neighbor. He wanted to see
for himself. I pointed to the towhee
cracking a sunflower seed.
"No," he said, pointing
to the coleslaw.

Be brave birders.
As in most matters of the heart,
you travel incognito,
and mostly you eat alone.

STEEL CUT

I try to avoid logic. It always takes me to where I've
already been and that's no fun. From there I head to
the two cups of water in the tap in the kitchen I have
yet to put in the pan to bring to a boil. Now I'm in
the kitchen with my arm around my mother's warm
leg anytime I want to go back there she appears. The
delicate scratching on the window is my morning
warbler. She comes to sing her song. I know my
rolling oats and her music are just for me. It's all about
entitlement, what rich people take for granted. I'm
not a cello but close. Together we get me in tune to
another day of senseless pleasure. So, about now add
the raisins, not too many or they'll swell too much
which is more poem than you want in your mouth.
Remember the Greeks—everything in proportion.
Writing poetry is the heart at war with the ordinary is
how I think about it so you have to get the flame
right. Of course birds come to me. There is no clear
separation between longing and warbler. What
more—a palm full of nuts. Your honey drizzled over
them.

GOING OUT

is me hanging over
the gunnels
watching the low level
drop of jellyfish,
their white canopies
float by tugging their lines.

Just not being in a hurry
to change directions
because someone on the radio
says, "the bites over here."

Oh bird, the knock
of your beak against the tree
that says "feed me."

The hummingbird
being god's tiniest
double ender,
does not really need
to turn around
backing out of the tulip.

We can't see the tiny crustaceans
that appear momentarily
when the surf
pulls the sand away,
but the hungry pipers can.

What we know for sure,
that between heaven and earth
there is a rub rail
that keeps us all here
in the slow going out,
and coming in.

BIRDERS

nationally,
except for Trappists,
are quieter
than the rest of us,
lighter
on their feet, too.
What's odd
is their uncommon
excitement
at just seeing
a bird, rare
or ordinary.
Arms start
waving
and legs
are inclined
to wobble
in some kind
of gratitude.
But if we think
of them
as a species,
these birders,
they're not

so endangered
as the monks
but they are
on the list
of those
most likely
to become so
owing to their
unguarded
enthusiasm.

Never mind.
Love them.
They might
just be
our last
best hope.

WHERE THE COUNTRY GOES WRONG

There are bluebirds
in our pancakes
my grandson points out
and with a smile
rolls one out with his finger.

The big Marine, with his broom,
in some secret facility
in Nebraska, Guam, the Philippines,
pushes it with real authority
in and around
the twenty-foot-long
nuclear bombs
lying in their silver aprons.

The bluebird is not a facility
is where the country goes wrong—
don'tcha see, words can kill us,
America?

Why won't they run the story
just once, that there's a proven
correlation between birdwatching
and peaceful co-existence?

Or do we need to know again
and again, front page,
that some politician's
been caught screwing his page?

The good news, though, the President
wants some quiet time
so he's put up a feeder,

and my grandson
breaks open his pancake
for another look inside.

CHRISTOPHER COLUMBUS DISCOVERS THE TAR SANDS OF ALBERTA

How did it happen
he got so far inside us?
You shave and you shave
and he still grows back
as wilderness caved in
under the iron shoes
of his horses.

The rumble we hear now,
the coming of giant modules
on flatbeds down our roads,
assaulting our towns,
our families.
They're not in the stars,
dear reader, but in ourselves,

and what's this new plan
500 years later
once they crawl their way to Alberta
on these mammoets?

We're going to build a fire,
then we're going to cook the earth
sick, 'til it pukes up its oil

and if we have to—
that's right you're in the kitchen
on this one, America—I mean if we have to

we'll deep-fry 160,000,000 wild fowl
and songbirds in summer
nurseries and nesting grounds.

How to save what's left?

Hard work.

You'll have to pull the Columbus in you
out from behind the wheel, America.

All good poems are hard work.

They say, *change your life,*

        change your life.

OUTSIDER ART

I'm making my own bird I've decided,
and he may not be pretty.
I've got the wire, and the temerity,
anyway, guts to jump in. I know how to bend
things to my liking. I'll need a lot of wire
like a Baskin crow just to carry his weight
with those balls he'll look us straight in the eye
without blinking and talk about what's his.

Jesus, a birder of parables,
never mentions the crow
in the six verses that only show us
in charge. I take a wider view:

the sun, each morning
fleshing out my Honey locust,
banging its yellow head into the suet,

old Matisse in his wheelchair,
cutting out paper birds,

the way the heart speeds up
on take offs and landings,

and that crow landing on the fantail
of the *USS Thetis Bay,* our ship
miles from land. Not a seagull, a crow,
then it walked right up to me.
I was eighteen, alone back there watching
the sea rise and fall behind us.

Wire's still cheap. The whole idea
is to make a bird you can believe in.
I'm working right now on the shoulders,
the head, where your eyes should go.

All this jabber. You can see I'm uncertain,
putting on feathers,
taking them off,

It's hard. If my grandsons were here
they'd know right away
the right colors for you.

Now your left eye's beginning to sag,
and you've got human knuckles for toes.
I know we started out with big plans
but you look more the outsider,
and with those balls,
you're too heavy to fly.

So much for our show of force.

In Rodin's studio there were drawers
full of little clay hands and broken feet.

Should I go back and start you over
(I know I've got the beak right)
bending my poem into a god?

WASN'T MY ARM A WING

You can't just say sparrow
and expect to get into heaven.
Doesn't work. Putting out seed either.
Though a bird close up might soften you.

When we hit a bird, there is the thud
of its small body against the grill,
the spray of feather, our cry and hand
trembling as it flies to our mouth.

That's a beginning.

Wasn't my arm a wing
I flapped when I was a boy,
both of them, trying to fly
off the chicken coop. I remember, too,
my long crawl across a field
of fresh cut alfalfa
cradling my first gun
to get in range of a meadowlark.

All our lives to learn the goldfinch
doesn't need us
but it'll eat our seeds.

Yet if we want to know what sky is,
or home, we have to look up,
and don't we have to put a bird in it.

Every kid, a god, knows this,
what's possible,
you only need a rubber band
to wind up the wings,
to get there.

ALL THE BIRDS ARE HERE

It's a noisy gathering
to wave us goodbye.
No hard feelings.
Just one reason, like dogs,
I so like birds:
they don't hold a grudge.
What a fine thing
to let go almost immediately
all the bad things
we've done to them.

You can see the bomb falling.
It's packed with all our good intentions.

The White-rumped Warbler
makes me smile.

If you want to get in here
you can add your bird now.

It's a damn shame, isn't it,
how our tool making
just got out of hand.

A word that kills: reclamation.
A word to love: waterbird.

Any bird can fly
rings around a rocket
and Mars is no wetland.

The contemplative bittern
lives down deep
in the reeds.
It's single croak,
when forced to fly,
"Leave me alone."

This is our "trail of tears,"
but not our Oklahoma.
Everything's used up
we might have called home.

HARRIET

One day Harriet
came to our feeder
(Mary named her Harriet)
Bird with a Green Hat,
Vermeer would say
a dapper bird
among the locals.

A bold, little parrot
in the wild
I would sing,
a bold little parrot
in the wild.

But then when
days went by
and no Harriet,
we kept quiet
our feelings
the big hole
at the feeder
you could crawl
in.

I couldn't help
though
but scan
the backyard
or on walks
in the neighborhood
look for the little pile
of Vermeer's
green
feathers.

Months, now,
what should we call it?
Our small loss,
a little parrot,

beauty, the way
it shakes the heart
out of its sleep.

THE MORANDI GAZE

ars poetica

Here he comes again Giorgio,
his whole life long climbing the same stairs.
Even downstairs, with his morning coffee,
reading the newspaper he'd be arranging
the empty vessels upstairs: this time the cracked
black bowl he thinks should go between the blue
jug and the squat white vase. This life, cordoned
off to see the shape of color could be my own
with millet and sunflower seeds. What's a feeder
hanging from the locust anyway, but longing.
Come birds I say and every time they arrange
themselves differently to show me color
is on the move.

SECTION II

I do not know which to prefer,
The beauty of inflections
Or the beauty of innuendoes,
The blackbird whistling
Or just after.

—WALLACE STEVENS

GREAT WORD

Dumbfounded,
like the feeling you get picking up
a single red feather
a little finch leaves behind
like some kind of care-package
dropped on you.

Or it's a stone, especially one of those
smooth, black ones
you hold to your ear
from a cold running creek
like Lolo that flows behind
my friends' house
in Montana. It's the operator
inside, telling you, go ahead,
you're connected.

Oh Lord of mine,
thank you for my slowness.
That I can't think faster
than snow falls,
or a feather.

Once on the Blackfoot

I saw myself from the other side,
the slide of dark water
around my waders,
the rod unloading
the wet line
unfolding toward me.

You know how in dreams
you get to fly? Everything's possible.
In mine I'm pretty as any bird.
Great word,
dumbfounded.

COMPANION TO A LOON

So you died, caught, I'll bet
in that gill net out there
held up by those big orange balls
stretched halfway across Tulalip Bay.
The Indian fisherman had to haul you up
then disentangle you
like so much stringy, green kelp.
It's unnatural that you should drown
that way, a perfect invention to water.
I'm sure I watched you the day before
yesterday, working the quiet shallows
around the boat dock
straight out from the little cabin.
Listen bird, I'm past making death sad.
The tide has no time for wakes
or tragedies. We're either coming in
or going out. It's like that,
the soul for a while boxed up
in feathers or this frail
human body of mine.
I'm just taking a little time out
from my walk because, well,
your drowned body is here
at my feet, even in death,
moving, unruffled.

HEAVY LIFTING

We are scared. It's accounting for things
that keeps dying manageable. The little bird
down there in the shadows, darting in and out
among the low branches over the pond,
moves too fast to name. But isn't that why
we've come, to make our lives a little more orderly,
and where being right or wrong doesn't matter?
What a blessing to know *The Sibley Guide to Birds*
will forgive us. To know the nuthatch from the flicker
doesn't pay the bills or make the Robocop
ticket less egregious, but getting the words
on our tongue swabs our wounds.
If birders on average live ten years longer
than just about everybody else, might it not
explain how we cover our mouths with our hands
and leave our bodies when a Cinnamon Teal
cruises out from the reeds. Birding is time out
from the heavy lifting of being who we are not.

GRAY LODGE

Every afternoon I close the door to my room and lie
down. For a while I will look at my hands. Even
though they are my hands, they are beautiful and I am
trying to work that out. When it is quiet enough I ask
my wife to look at me. She's dead, but what does that
mean. It's new for both of us and hard but I'm not
afraid of work. If there are birds in the yard we begin
there the old way. Every bird counts for something,
we believe, like the camera giving you a picture
of light or happiness. Once at Gray Lodge we
watched a thousand snow geese rise up off the water.
And when one lifts up, they all lift up. It's plain that
geese love each other. But still, in my room, I lock my
thumbs together to make a goose, to make a goose cry.
Sometimes I wish I were stronger. Then I could say,
"It's raining by God but I have these houses to build."
Then the world, the world would fall in place like the
carpenter's trilogy. Every sixteen inches another joist,
nailed, on center. But no...in here it is quiet. So quiet
we don't need to see each other to know. When you
live like that there are no houses. Birds come inside.
They fly right through you.

HALF A BUDDHA

The dead bird
leaves its feathers
for next spring's nest.

Don't grow up
to never bend
down
for one.

The sun's
in the window.
The birds
are already up.

Get outside
me is such a heavy
coat to wear.

CROP CIRCLES

Billy, we didn't know
we couldn't fool it,
that the vulture's
sense of smell
would tell it
we were not dead,
just two little boys,
lying perfectly still
in the pasture
with their bow
and arrows.

Wilderness on one side,
pasture on the other.
I learned early to just wait
for the quail
to come to me
out of the manzanita,
ducking their blue heads
under the barbwire fence,
always a big male in the lead,
its plume tossing.

It was for the family.
It wasn't sport. I was a hungry
Natty Bumppo
so one shot
for the kill
fed us all.

On-call is okay
but to attend
is better,
is to care for
the fatally injured
Blue Swallow,
its mate staying with it
the whole time,
beside the highway,
'til the end.

Goodbye Mountain Bluebird,
Snowy Plover, Clapper Rail.
Look at what we've done
to you, to our language:
Habitat, decline, endangered species,
extinct, don't mean a thing,

do they, unless someone's
bulldozing
your house?

Jim Claffey who just died, used to fly
B52s high over Cambodia. "We probably hit
more parrots than gooks."

Like the pinched candlelight
their song gone out.

One is okay, one white bird skull
you can hold between the thumb
and index finger.
It's a beautiful thing.
As a kid I'd get high
on gasoline,

and pop quizzes
always made my hands sweat.
Name five birds
for a fill up. Remember to put your name
in the upper right hand corner
of your paper.

Impossible to talk survival
and not be ironic.

I would have flown that bomber
in a heartbeat
when I was twenty-five,
and I was a nice young man, too.

I still love the lighted refineries,
the rank smell of them
when I drive by,
the luminous columns of steam
rising up at night
like I'm there at Cape Canaveral
just before liftoff.
Possible answers:

Red-breasted Nuthatch,
Hermit Thrush,
White-crown Sparrow,
Curved-bill Thrasher,
Cooper Hawk.

For extra credit:
What song were they singing,
the doomed ones
on the top deck
of the Titanic
when it went under?

I was like you,
a believer
in the Skilsaw,
Bubble Wrap,
the Microchip.
If they said buy
I bought.
Before the game
my hand flew
like yours
up to my heart.
The roar
of the Blue Angels
sweeping
over the football stadium
went right through me.
Guns, I had three.
A twelve gauge
Winchester,
just for target practice.
Birds? No, all my birds
were made of cardboard.

It's a Mannlicher,
Wall Street,

the way it fits
the shoulder
on the opening bell,

a shot bird
that flaps
along
the ground
with its one good wing,

while at Yellowstone
magma swells
the dome
and spring
swallows
carry
warm mud
balls
in their beaks.

Its chatter/song—you
tell me—sounds like water
boiling in a beat up
aluminum pot.
The raven doesn't know
either, that it's a raven.

Down below the tree,
Homo erectus. Are we
a conundrum
it bends its head toward:
two legs, no wings,
making guttural sounds,
charmed by our own similes?

Yes, yes, impermanence.
Better sing now,
Tom, the winter
plum tree
outside the window,
a case in point,
its trunk black as a tire
pulled to a stop in the snow,
will soon be moving on.

The left hand
flat over the fingers
of the right hand,
fingers together
pointing up
means the clock's
running out,
means we're using up

all our time outs.

Nobody's too big
for dying. Thomas Jefferson,
a birder, too,
took great pleasure
his last day on earth,
(too weak to leave his bed),
when a tiny Crown Sparrow
peered in at him
through the window.

An invisible wind sweeps
the bare branches. No matter
how tight the window,
cold gets in, a silver whistle
in its mouth.

RELEASE AT NETARTS BAY

We carry the bird in a cardboard box
through low tide
and a hundred yards of ancient mud
to the edge of the water
just when the sun is going down
and the light makes us feel
suddenly happy.

In this old mud there is hope,
the loon stirring to the rich smell,
salt air, and lap of water.
He knows the world
of going down
and which fish are his
then coming up after
always in a different place.

In moving he is always home.

This is all we want,
a chance for the walk out,
our hands wet like this
when we let him go.

But my country, what do you want,
so in love with the straight line
the bird will never take.

Call this our letter.

I ask for both of us: friends,
respectfully, weaving through mud
toward another order.

ROOSEVELT'S DIARY

talks about how a little sparrow
in Wyoming
did him in,
landing on the great man's saddle
on a hunting trip in 1880.

Most men
(we don't really know why),
aren't moved by birds.
Some kind of wall
the bird crashes into
like hitting the slider
to the patio, the body, feathers—
a small sadness
that one sweeps away.

But for a few, like Teddy,
it's different. The bird comes inside.

It could have been a clean shot,
he said, the bull elk no more than 200 yards
away, standing broadside
in a grove of aspen.

"I could not aim the damn gun, silly as that might
sound,
let alone pull the trigger while this little bird was
perched
on the horn of my saddle. His soul, so tiny, I believed,
was visiting mine."

Some things you just can't make up.
His love, too, of the Powder River
he camped by that night.

Or his favorite gun, he called "big medicine,"
the 405 Winchester, lever action, kept wrapped
in an oiled chamois until just before
he mounted his horse.

To hold it against your warm cheek
the cherry stock,
the soft grain,
the smell of it,
and just before it goes off.

A muzzle velocity they knew about
but couldn't measure in his day.
Always Krishna's man,

so in war Teddy took the long view.
He had no trouble killing a hundred men
to worry ten thousand.

The little sparrow gone in a flash,
that charming visitation
held sacred, he talked about
for years after.

Six children, twenty-two grandchildren,
twice that many great-grandchildren,
but to Teddy's disappointment
not a poet among them.

Few close friends.
Quiet was the best conversation
he liked to say except talking
about wild things. A mountain,
he could gaze on for hours, or a river,
sitting on its bank.

A Killdeer runs a few feet
in the shallows, stops, bobs
up and down while a little breeze
unsettles a couple feathers.

Its song, dee dee, dee dee,

words,
that's what he had and the clear water
they drank from.

WHAT'S CHRISTMAS TO A BIRD

Not much. Though the bare peach tree
in front of our kitchen window
might as well be a Christmas tree
the way they hang there
from the snow-heavy branches.
The finches, of course, the brightest
bulbs. It's a handy perch this little tree,
the feeder so close by.

Who in the neighborhood
clangs the invisible dinner bell
that calls them in? Snow
dissolves most class lines. The dove sits
with the Oregon Junco.
Even the big thrasher, ordinarily an eater
of insects, shoulders its way in
to wolf down the black
sunflower seeds.

It's a nervous feed, though. Every bird
with a tic. They just want to live.
The flicker adorns the tree
with its salt and pepper feathers.
An easy target for the hawk,
still, it pulls at the suet.

There are so many ways to die.
Dharma cut off his eyelids
in order to be alert, to miss nothing.

What's Christmas to a bird—
these luminous birds—me,
carrying my bucket of seeds,
through the snow.

SPOTTER SCOPE

With only binoculars I couldn't be sure
it was the Long-billed Curlew,
half a mile away and rare, feeding
in the shallow water below the mudflat—
just slender stilts under a pumpkin belly.

A strong wind ruffles the lake in the spotter scope,
and with the slightest jar you lose the bird.

We try not to push as we line up to take our turns
to peer across. "Yes, it has the long bill and look,
now you can see how it curves down," Tom says,
our leader for this outing.
Then adds, "and there are the grey legs."

Rick, my friend, is ahead of me. For twenty-three
years he's fixed computers
for 165 employees working in tiny cubicles
at the Justice Department in Santa Fe.

The wind whips a big cottonwood by the road,
showering our cars with yellow leaves.
Someone lifts a hand to catch one.
We're mostly oldsters out here on the preserve

with our lunches, books, binoculars.

A mile south a huge quarrel going on.
What Snow Geese sound like on take-off.

One man with scarcely any hair, big smile,
lifts his head from the scope to claim he once
saw a godwit up close in Puget Sound.

RAIN

Heavy rain all morning.
But nothing much
can rouse the eagle
from its perch
atop the barnacle
encrusted black pile,
but a couple of crows try
with a barrage of caws
dives and wing flapping
before they fly off.
My binoculars
bring the bird up close.
It turns toward me.
Water drips
from its hooded eyes.

PIGEON GUILLEMOT

February 20, and I would like to think
that I saw them first, coming ashore.
I don't mean walking but rather,
the way they do, first picking themselves up
out of the surf, altogether determined,
then aiming their small, black bodies
at the holes and crevices in the high cliffs,
half the time aborting the mission
halfway there or after discovering
another auk already inside.
Unable to hover, they only get one shot.
Then back to the water to consider
where they went wrong. Think
blood-red rhubarb
and you have the color of their feet,
splayed out in front of them for the landing.
It's not beauty though, but failure
I most connect with. Like the feathered
equivalent of the little engine that could,
back one goes, to a different hole this time,
tumbling in. You could call it play,
the thing they have to do and why shouldn't they,
having come this far, throw themselves into it?

CRACKED CORN

From my front porch in winter
I throw a little cracked corn
to the world.
Who can beat the sparrows in,
all flit and scatter and return,
pecking their way around the feet
of the domestics: chickens, ducks,
and the big bombers, our geese
who come rolling up, mostly to bully.
There are pleasures in distribution:
where the leaves fall,
the assignment of heron to water
back of the house.
My love of windows, this habit
of looking out I have, now
into cold February.
Who can imagine a better life?
The day, quiet, just invented,
the start of crocus.

REDWING

He's inside my mouth,
no, beside the road
clinging to a May cattail.
It gets confusing, what's in,
what's out, like saying the sun's up
or down when we know it's none of those
and words, even the good ones,
can only pepper the edge
of feelings and that's what we're after
here which means going down
the throat to get to where he lives.
But if I start smiling because
there's a bird inside me
you can guess how long I'd be allowed
out, alone. So, like a few others,
to remain free I play that down
when pointing to a world
that's not supposed to be
which only means
they've been piling rocks on me
for years—an old Puritan trick—to get me
to come around to their god.
I must be Buddhist. The bell
has its own words for it—water, wind,
the quiet world a bird brings.

AM I MY FEET

Okay, when I close my eyes in order to feel my feet,
then ask myself the question, "Am I my feet?" right away,
comes the answer: "No, you are not your feet."
You can see, can't you, where this is going?
It'll be the same answer, no matter
what part of my body I query. Even something
as close to me as my penis, which, over the years
I've shown so much attention to
the answer comes back, nada.
Does this mean I'm essentially invisible?
That the huge black raven in the park today,
bowlegged, walking through the snow,
was not really there either? Lord, take my penis
if you have to—it's been a pain
right along anyway, but not the beautiful raven.
Not the claw prints trailing behind him
under the warm, winter sun. Not the coarse kraaah.

"TENDER YOUR RESIGNATION"

my hands say, with their swelled veins.
It's true, there is nothing here that wasn't issued,
wouldn't expect to be returned. Struggle is useless.
The bird once caught in the cat's mouth
does not fight it. And entitlement, what's that—
the drained reds of autumn, someone
having fun with us. How to bend down and take off
your worn shoes for the last time or somehow let go
the grip on the hammer, handyman? Everything
is love, renovation, biscuits, and gravy.

PRAYER

I'm cutting my swallows from black silk,
China's best, Father, so that when flying
they meet with the least amount of resistance
and thank you again for the abundance
of insects over the green rice fields
this evening, the water bumpy with frog eyes
reflecting a pink west-flowing sky.

Now I'm sewing into the material
my red heart because the dead lately
have been a little noisy in my sleep
and about this prayer, Father,
I don't want any confusion—

I'm mud deep here in love
and would like to stay on
a while longer, at least until I get the sun right,
its light over the rim of this bowl
we all eat from, and to watching,
while I'm at it, the little spot fires
appearing over the backs of my hands,

my age, a quiet invitation
to bird watching

where light around the Gray Heron,
alone in the water,
dies down, in time, to black
and what the imagination can rescue.

BIRD WALK IN CHINA

Old age and freedom,
so long in coming
they can hardly stay awake for it
these retired Party members
who sometimes doze off in the morning sun
down in Lieschimu
their arms around their caged birds.
I look inside to see what it is they love so much.
This brown headed, solitary bird
with green eye lids,
inimical to ruffled feathers seems to know
its company, alone, is enough.
If it moves at all I can't tell,
it's such a fine adjustment in color.
By its gold knuckled toes
it maintains center on a single perch.
Moved by my interest,
the old men always smile to see me coming.
One points to the new door he's added—
a tiny bamboo grove etched in thin bronze.
He is especially happy about the blue-green patina
I trace with my finger.
Each has his own logo
written in Chinese over the entrance.

Blue Cloud Gate on one. Cold Mountain
on another. What's standardized here?
That the men all be old.
That the cages look like cages
and the small doors, whatever their design,
open inward.

WU WEI

Walk the same beach enough
and widgeon stay put,
gulls too. You become common
like bullwhip washed up
or broken soft-shell.
Driftwood becomes you,
sitting for hours alone,
reciting the sutra of doing nothing.
What's more exciting than a wind shift,
a patch of green water close by,
its back suddenly up, a surprise riff
running against the tide.
You can't think your way to anything
around water this old.
The Talmud, Bible,
it doesn't matter, won't stack up
to the invisible column of air
eagles ride or water
lapping ordinary light. A beach
after a while just grinds you down
to quiet, where words—even the good ones,
the fuss they make—won't last.
Yes, yes, I'm here. Look at me.
Resolved. My broken walking stick
writing the names of those I love
in the sand.

SECTION III

*Birds are holes in heaven through which
a man may pass.*

—WALTER ANDERSON, *Horn Island Diaries*

ARRHYTHMIA

My history? Maybe it was always there,
doctor, my irregular heartbeat
but I only became aware of it
the first time I heard the Hermit Thrush.
That's right. But I'd have to go back years
to Kern County, me behind the wheel
of an old, red Buick, engine gone,
car up on blocks, next to a creaking oil well.
It was west of our farm out in the desert.
My legs barely reached the pedals.
I had the window rolled down
to hear the wind, the sand
pepper the fenders, the windshield.
I was happiest alone, leaving home
on my imaginary wheels.

That bird, its song, a long, sad note
fading away out in the sage, beyond the oily
drums, the pump house.

In those days, doctor, an angel followed me
everywhere. We explored the abandoned wells.
Piles of steel casings gone to rust. Mean, black cable—
paint brush growing up through the coiled

knots—where horny toads lived.
Wooden derricks, some still standing,
polished to silver from a hundred years
of wind and sand. We could be so quiet
out there rabbits would come out of hiding for us.

I saw the little thrush only once, years later,
black dots on its chest. Such a shy bird.
Ornithologists call its song
a 'soft whistle.' But there is no song
without affliction, doctor. No bird, if we'll listen,
that does not build its secret nest in us
out of old string and dead feathers.

THE NAMES OF BIRDS

Getting the names of birds after sixty
turns into some kind of race. You still can't see
the finish line—it's not that bad or good—
but now you know it's up there. So, when Gary slowed
the little pickup outside of Manchester
to point out to me the Greater Scaup
with its stunning blue bill,
water bubbling off as it pulled up beach kelp,
I was surprised. Even more at my immediate feelings
of, what can I say, envy, the way he got there first
and with so much authority, the name, the way
he already owned it. You couldn't exactly see
the flag he'd planted in that gorgeous bird's
back, but it was there all right. Maybe I got even,
if that doesn't sound too tit for tat,
when I introduced him to my humble
little Pied-billed Grebe in its winter plumage
on a walk by Tulalip Bay.
I babbled on a bit and being less than gracious
I think I immediately repeated the name,
like I was Shackleton discovering the South Pole.
What gets into us after sixty that has us
slowing down at the same time we're speeding up?
Birds know it. We're not coming with a gun.

That each one has a name and we're out to learn it,
well, that's a human thing. There's always going to be
the urgency toward the end
and we've got a lot of birds to go.

IT HANDS OUT THE GOLD

Was it light or the owl
who named the barn?
It gets confusing.
What a swift glide
it makes on last darkness
into the hay loft,
straight for the cobwebs, rafters,
as light again makes the barn.
The dark shapes below it,
cows, horses. A water trough.
That old trick again—the sun
on a roll. All things we love.
The bad dreams
morning shakes off,
the darkness in our pockets.

FEEDER

Early morning
in the dark
I can't see myself.

I'm where
I'm supposed to be
though,
in my chair
quiet,
listening to a wing
flutter
against the window.

An old man
putting out seed
for more than birds.

NOT BEING A GOD

Pain's good. I know that
though I don't get up in the morning
and say, "Hurt me."
The sunlight in the double sinks,
the fresh brown eggs by the stove, leaning
into each other and the thick, pepper bacon,
these are sources of pleasure. Buddha
in the kitchen, cooking breakfast.
But not being a god, like me He's clumsy
and allows a spoonful of hot grease
to splash on my hand. What to do
after the scream I figure
is why we're here.

A little more every day
two baby finches dissolve
into the planter
under the window
where they've fallen
after the big storm.

Not pretty to look at,
what the hot grease did to my skin.

I could have walked out the door
when the wind was blowing
so hard that day, discovered the little birds
and put them back in the nest.
But I didn't. Or I didn't notice.

Loss, yes, it's beautiful,
the poem with all the nails in it.
Who says cooking's pleasant
with its assortment of knives,
the bleating lamb chop.

By now I know all the charming
metaphors for Zen mind.
All the traps.

Even the seven story Buddha
that greeted me all those years ago
when I came around the corner
in the village of Kamakura.
C'mon!

Holding on to the grab-iron
when the ship pitches,
pissing gonorrhea, the urethra on fire
is another way of knowing.

One light in the kitchen.
My little ritual,
to just be here,
and warm my hands
on the hot steam
from the espresso.

Night, goose down,
dreams. We are all water,
water and dreams.
The earth abides,
never a drop lost.

ON THE BACK SIDE OF A CEMETERY
IN SANTA FE, NM

The Teddybear cactus didn't come here
to soothe us.In color it's a dusty gray
and always in a state of shedding some part
of itself, an arm, a leg while all the time
it's growing a new one. It figured out long ago
how not to die completely. The discarded body
parts, mostly holes now, the exoskeleton
you can carry home to study
the mysteries of emptiness.

But if you'll just be quiet for a moment,
the Curved-bill Thrasher, gray too,
will now performs its disappearing act: it hovers
a moment above her gorgeous yellow blooms
then drops down suddenly
into the thousand needles
where somewhere inside it built its nest.

What more proof of the resurrection
then on the back side of a cemetery—soft trills
and warbles from this bristling podium
of an un-huggable Teddybear.

ONE BIRD WORKS FOR A WHILE

I was born to birds,
what's gold in the wing
on takeoff,
and makes a little hole
in the sky my eyes can follow.

One bird works for a while.

What container ship
can compare,
weighed down,
bloated,
that needs a mile to turn
around, unlike the egret

dropping in
to the mud flat
on cupped wings

it warms me
all the way down
to water.

I get, on average,

ten minutes
out of a landing

but over the years
it adds up.

It's what you can pocket
that matters.

YELLOW-BREASTED CHAT

"Don't stop coloring," he said,
my skulking uncle
who one day in Michigan
disappeared forever
in a field of corn.

Before that you could name a bird
and he'd tell you the family,
habitat, then mimic its song.

To the label, idiot savant,
he'd flap his make-believe wings,
and crow, "Impaired,
we're all impaired."

The chat right now
hangs upside down
from our arbor
plundering a black cluster
of grapes.

Whatever I tell you
you can believe me the poem
won't lie. Only birds get in

and my skulking uncle.

Once, when I was a boy
I brought him a dead bird. "Here,"
he said, putting it to my nose,
"smell freedom."

Believe, don't believe
what the chat brings,

that he's found the secret peach
hidden in the foliage
and he's standing on it now,
pulling up the red skin.

THE CHINESE MIGHT SAY, THERE IS NO TEA IN YOU

or no bird. Same thing. This is a problem
for the country. What's real. Well,
when two black socks on the clothesline
turn into two crows chewing the fat,
you've opened the door. And remember,
it's not about what's real. Go there
and you carry a stun gun. Staying in charge
you forget the poor. Bird watching
is the color of hope. Like writing poetry,
you have to believe in what's not there
until it is. So it doesn't matter that your crows
were really ravens, but only that you
stayed put long enough to notice
they were birds at all, or black socks. So
what if you get the bird wrong or its song,
or that at night you confuse the owl's
luminous eyes with the moon
sitting on a high branch in your oak tree.
Theory is not the issue, or particle physics,
but that you're out there, alone, in the cold
without a sweater on. Slow down
when you make tea for the bird
inside who says let's take the day off.
We're going to go see ourselves up close.
Wear a warm jacket. Grab your binoculars.

IN ORDER TO LET THE SOUL OUT SOONER

Tibetan monks
would chop us up
into manageable
chunks
for the vultures.

Good for the birds
who also have to eat
and for the earth
which will have us,
one way or the other.

I like the idea
that one of my old hands
might fly off
into the Himalayas
in the beak of bird
with an eight foot
wingspan.

How the soul figures
finally, in all this
is anybody's guess.
Just that it comes out

more readily,
the monks believe,
with every whack
of the blade.

I like being
parsed out this way
I have to say,
the great birds
squabble
over me, too.

We are all food
for the gods
as we fly
to the next life.

CELLO

My friend likes to say, "Of course, you're a poet."
This always in response to my feelings,
then he smiles. He's right.
To eat to stay alive isn't good enough.
An old lesson in aesthetics: the chicken wings
have to hurt you too
or who cares.

⟋

Joy, when it lasts, is always a dark licorice. Look!
The Chrysler Building at night, topped off
in silver scallops. Beautiful. Yes,
but there's nothing there to make us sweat
under the covers.

⟋

Geese on water, what a pretty sight.
But it won't last, no. It's the one with the broken wing
pushing itself in a circle, the despair of its mate.
The end of hope is what we learn by heart.

⟋

What's sad is what we've come for.
The bare, lighted stage.

Four strings and a wooden box
where one note can turn over in us
the deepest soil.

TO REMEMBER, AGAIN, WHAT'S GOOD

*"Let one by one things come alive like fish
and swim away into their future waves."*
—William Stafford

Seven-years-old-gone-mother.
It's spring. You're in the shallow water
just off the bank of the Nestucca River
near the Riverhouse, (do you remember?),
with your sweet, grownup ducks in a box.

They're quacking, both of them, excited
by the smell of water and the wild ducks
across the river, quacking back.

It's a brave moment for all of us
when you let them out.

Oh, they're beside themselves
your ducks, with love for you,
the big river, as they paddle out several feet
into the deep water toward that call
then back to you, your hands
stroking their wet heads.

From the bank we look at you,
our daughter, bent down
in the sunlight, in the river,
your darlings swimming
in confused circles around you.

And then it happens. They paddle out
again, further this time, glance back,
and with the clamber of the wild ducks
like a pair of invisible scissors
over the water, the connection's cut
and off they go, half paddling, half flying.

Hardly feathered dots now on the big river
while you strain to follow them across.
Such a commotion of quacks
and wing flapping, water flying,
as they're gathered in
on the other side.

GRACKLE

A Monty Python bird,
(who else could have
dreamed you up?),
mostly rudder,
you row your ridiculous
boat of common
black feathers
across the Texas sky,
carefully, so as
not to capsize
on somebody's lawn
or in the Safeway parking lot
as you struggle
from cottonwood
to laurel.

It gets worse. *The Sibley*,
(Bible to birdwatchers)
describes your song
as "a harsh, toneless,
metallic hiss."

How to fly in the world
with so much against you?

If there are bully birds around,
I'm sure you know them too.

Maybe you've come here
enchanted the way we have
with this vast, quiet prairie
of candle plants, few people,
the Marfa lights?

No matter
your hiss, dear blackbird,
is my bell,
to you I dedicate
all my unsteady poems.

RAPTOR

One who seizes. *Bird of prey.*

Yes, yes, it's true, it eats other birds.

A little narrative: Picasso, my bantam rooster,
lost his head to a Red-tailed Hawk in Oregon
in 1987
and it happened so fast, he instantly got back up
and walked around, headless, shaking
the dust out of his green feathers.

Rodin could think in stone. He knew how to push
in and out, deep folds, big shoulders, and the
gazing eyes for Balzac's beak.

Being a romantic, I thought, what a way to go,
god takes your head off on a sunny day in the pasture.
And look what you're feeding?

I stayed in the house, heart pounding. It was his kill.

So much to love. So little time.

Never mind the guard at the Met

who doesn't want you to touch him,
eight-foot Balzac. You might think he was dangerous,
in his black bronze.

Would I, if I could, save Picasso?
No, I don't think so. I'm more witness,
and this is beauty from longing
torn.

THE PRESIDENT'S LAST SPEECH

We could do
bombs,
but we couldn't do
birds,
couldn't learn
to sing
even one
little titmouse
out of hiding.

The smart boys
only got right
probability,
translated:
fat chance
this bus
will ever come
our way
again.

If birds are gods
then I believe in god.

Let's be happy
though,
with our absence:
the earth will
still pull on its pants
every morning

and birds
(can you imagine
their chatter?)
will do nicely
without us.

WHAT LASTS

Say Chopin
and mean wren,
mean sunlight
through the snow–
powdered window,
crumpled sheets
at the foot of the bed
or their joy
at first seeing
the little bird
looking in,
pecking at the glass.
What lasts?
Chopin,
looking
for his shorts,
wanting more
than anything
now
his buttered
biscuits,
tea,
his piano.

TO GO VERY SOFTLY

Photograph by Jean-Luc Mylayne

We get the blue sky
don't we,
and the almost leafless
gray branch
and near its center
a red bird
perched, not sure
but probably a warbler,
its small heart
pumping out
a warm aura
and a song
that swells its chest.

What is it
then that flies inside us
we can't name
so call beauty?

We're down here
on the ground.
It's what we have

to work with

and time
and the fire's
last click.

THE PIE IS *NOW*

It's silly to talk to the peach tree
about future pies, that's why
we have portfolio managers
for those who want to get ahead
which can be hell on a good night's sleep.
Birds ease into the morning,
they take it one sunrise at a time. Einstein
was interested in the future
but said the speed of light being constant,
we'd have to live into it.
For the Black-headed Grosbeak,
who's in my fruit tree
the pie is now. So I'm learning to live
into seventy-one with a bird
whose only plan is flying
between peaches.

RAVEN

One story has it we flew in here
on the backs of birds. Ravens to be exact.
They still don't hold us in high regard,
our fear of wilderness, our urban gods,
our flush toilets. They seem to know
we won't last. As the intermediaries
between heaven and earth, they hang out
in our neighborhoods. It's their job.
They perch on telephone poles, wires,
the tops of trees. They peer down at us
who are stuck to the earth in shoes
that follow the same old sidewalks,
roads, day in day out. Case in point:

A woman in her backyard is hanging
a red dress on the clothesline when two
ravens drop down to the roof of the garage
to have a closer look. Then they begin
making boisterous chortling sounds,
all the time their heads pumping up and down.

"Harry, come outside," she hollers,
"look at this." She, excited-scared.
"Harry, hurry!" she pleads. Harry

comes out the back door, then shakes
his head in disbelief. "For fuck sake, Louise,
they're just crows," he says, and goes back inside.

My mind today is half a bucket
of blue latex paint I've stretched across the wall
of our storage shed. I'm like Pollock now,
holding my drip stick, waiting for my ride.

THE SPILL

"We're in deep shit," the foreman yells
when the form splits open and we all watch
the river of cement pour out
across the ground.

Some things can't be saved.

Let's say it was a rush job, our evolution.

The Brown Pelican didn't take part
in the Industrial Revolution.
It just wanted to go on being a pelican.

Unable to fly, it waddles down the beach
dragging its useless *dip net*
while the ocean serves up more tarballs
and plastic spoons.

You want a happy poem,
everything to be put back right?
That was the Romantic period.

Even as we sleep
and dream our dreams,
ships are dragging their black nets
along the floors of the ocean.

OWNERSHIP

I own my house and my old teeth,
they belong to me, too. And the gun
leaning in the corner, that's mine.
And the Barn Owl, dead,
still tumbling through the air
out of the palm tree
in Bakersfield when I was a boy,
the sound it made hitting the ground
at my feet, and the speckled
white feathers that broke from the wings.

How dangerous youth is,
from owl to war with hardly
a break in between.

The wake behind our carrier
where daily we threw out
all our garbage. How did I survive
the violence of those years?

Bad uncles
who could only talk knockers and guns,
my angry father
who called Jews kikes and Blacks, niggers.

It's like secondhand smoke;
you can still die from it.

Nothing's disparate in here. All mine.
A Rauschenberg, my owl alive to
the touch, coming out of the torn
matting, cigarette tinsel, smeared oils.

BOSQUE DEL APACHE

Birders are like old monks
from another life,
still in formation,
still shy. They
can't seem to break the habit
of silence, to rise early,
to hope.

They gather in the cold
by a lake and then
just stand there, quietly
and stare out
into the darkness.

They love what can't be
improved on,
first light, bird song,
the perfect hydraulics
of the cranes' legs
that fold back
in a shower of water
as their great wings
lift them all
into the morning sky.

Among these curious,
no reckless enthusiasm.
(It's not a football game.)
The older ones, too frail
for the cold,
watch from their cars
until the birds are out of sight.

That's it.

The lake water still trembling,
but empty.

One or two
might have taken pictures,
their only show
of attachment.

CANARY

The canary in the coal mine has turned
into the common Barn Swallow,
its dazzling flight over trees,
under bridges. The sky its commissary.
In parts of the country it's starving to death:
blame our ingenuity, the pretty
red crop duster.

James Wright saw it coming,
Ohio, 1977: "It turns out/
You can kill them./It turns out/
You can make the earth
Absolutely clean."

Hope. That the soup kitchen
on 39th and Fillmore will be open.
Across the street an old man
preaches the end of the earth.
Hopelessness? No birds in this poem.
Nothing in here but hunger.
People on the street look away,
they won't read a homeless poem.

THE GOOD RED ROAD

And furthermore
do not let me,
god, wither,
or the woodpecker
not stop me
cold in my tracks
with its laddered
back.

Truth be told,
before there were glazes,
Jesus drank
bad wine
out of a low fire,
cracked pot.

And the wily coyote,
we can't get enough
of him, his ups
and downs,
he suffers
so much abuse.

On the good, red road

though, there's a resident poet
in every stone,
and an Indian pony
eats out of your hand.

Now I lay me down
to sleep. Beside the still waters
cranes put the seal of their long toes
in the mud

and dying is just swinging out
over the big river,
then letting go.

Let's do it.

ACKNOWLEDGMENTS

Many people were involved directly and indirectly in the evolution of this book and I want to thank them all. But three friends immediately come to mind who I especially want to note for their contributions. George Manner, always gracious, a Southern boy from Louisiana. I still see us sitting across from one another in our wooden booth at Tia Sophia's in Santa Fe, where every Monday we'd meet for burritos and a quiet place to gab about poetry. There's hardly a poem in here that George, himself a poet extraordinaire, has not made better through his nudges and suggestions. So it should be no surprise to the reader that I express my grief at losing my dear friend to cancer last October. Then there's Mary Judge, also a gifted writer. From the get-go she's been my unofficial editor and critic. In a real sense she deserves the most praise since as my partner too, living in the same small house, she's been unable to escape my daily obsession. "Mary," I'd say, striding into the dining room where she'd be trying to enjoy her morning coffee, *The New York Times*, a little solitude, "listen to this." Gary Thompson, the last in this triumvirate. He's allowed me to batter him for months, years, with many of these same bird poems; Gary Thompson who actually began reading my work long ago while we were both graduate students. Gary, who's the birder in the title poem. Cunning comes to mind, the nuanced way he has of assessing a poem, then showing me how it might break out into something larger.

But my gratitude also extends to others who have contributed mightily to *The Names of Birds*: David James Duncan whose quixotic spirit in life and in the foreword to these poems has emboldened me to charge a few windmills of my own. Jim Harrison, because in the sheer inventiveness of his poems, their originality, I've found so much inspiration for my own. Quinton Duval, old, dear friend and poet, who left us last year. I miss his late night phone calls, his playful insults, his take on a new bird poem, then him saying, "Well, Tom let's close up for the night with a little old song," as he'd launch into a renditions of "Candy Kisses" by Lefty Frizzell. Judyeth Sieck, for her talent, her buoyancy, support that has culminated in the lovely design of the jacket and the book. Richard Kehl, for the nuanced and lovely bird image on the cover. Pattiann Rogers, for her careful reading of the poems and fine cover endorsement. Burke Denman, my silent partner who in the course of many lunches (always his treat) would ask me, somewhere after the arrival of the entrée: "Ok, now tell me, how's the book coming?" Thomas Keith, my New York editor who more than once could see into the book more than I could, what it wanted to be. Amazing. And thank you, Jim Mafchir, my publisher, who endured all my cantankerousness. Some of the support comes in less demonstrative ways, but no less important to me. Krystal Wirfs, for example, an old friend who months back when we were getting into the car in Portland, Oregon, turned to me and announced to all of us in the car her affection, admiration for my life, putting poetry ahead of all else. Then, just to make sure I got the point, she said, "I mean it, Tom." My sister, T.J. Christenson, whose support for my poetry has flowed like a river over the years. Sarah Phelan and Sue Lyons—I send them poems, they send back boxes of fresh lemons from their own tree, which in our kitchen I'd turn into lemon tarts, to die for. Siegfried Halus, for his companionship, cheap Scotch, and splendid photograph of me for the back cover. For my grandsons, Aidan and Lael, who already understand that a life without poetry and art is unthinkable.

ABOUT THE AUTHORS

Tom Crawford is the author of five previous books of poetry, and the recipient of the Pushcart Prize, ForeWord Book of the Year, the Oregon Book Award for Poetry (Lauds), and two National Endowment for the Arts Fellowships.

David James Duncan is recipient of a Lannan Literary Fellowship (2002). National Book Award Finalist for *My Story as Told by Water*, 2001. Best known for his two best-selling novels, *The River Why* and *The Brothers K*. Both received the Pacific Northwest Booksellers award, *The Brothers K* was a *New York Times* Notable Book in 1992 and won a Best Books Award from the American Library Association.

COLOPHON

This book was created using using Quark XPress.
The text is Bembo with headings in Cresci and the
display typeface is Gill Sans Light

Edited by Thomas Keith
Interior and cover design by Judythe Sieck
Cover image by Richard Kehl
Typesetting and production by Jim Mafchir
Printed in USA